The New Yorker's Guide to Collaborative Divorce

Second Edition

By Katherine Eisold Miller, JD

The New Yorker's Guide to Collaborative Divorce

Second Edition

By

Katherine Eisold Miller, JD

The Miller Law Group

Table of Contents

__Introduction__

Sarah and Matthew had been married for 18 years when Matthew confessed to Sarah one evening that he was seeing another woman. Sarah was stunned, hurt and angry. Sarah, like many other people in similar situations didn't know what to do. She was worried about her three young sons, terrified about money, and disoriented. Her friends and relatives urged her to protect herself and see a lawyer right away. Several names and business cards of well-regarded attorneys in her area were sent her way and one day she came to see me.

When Sarah and I met she was distraught. When we started talking she confessed to me that her marriage had not been perfect by any means. She had been busy with the kids for years and Matthew had a job in the City where he worked long hours. They had grown apart and— although they both enjoyed their children— they had come to live parallel lives. Their intimate life had suffered and Sarah told me that for a little over a year Matthew had often slept in a spare bedroom. They didn't fight but they also weren't close. Nonetheless, Sarah had thought they were fine, not that different from other couples she knew, and Matthew's confession had taken her by surprise.

Sarah's story is similar to many other stories I hear frequently. Sarah came to see me in the midst of a swirl of emotions: anxiety, fear, shame, anger mixed with some relief. She didn't want the divorce, but she didn't want to be married to someone who didn't want to be with her. She didn't even know what a divorce involved or what her choices were.

That day I listened to Sarah's story and started working with her to think about the decisions and choices she had coming in the following days, weeks and months. The first choice she had was the decision of how she and Matthew were going to go about resolving the problems they faced as a divorcing couple. Were they going to try to work it out themselves alone at home, were they going to hire lawyers and move toward litigation, or did they want support to guide and facilitate the necessary conversations either in mediation or Collaborative Law? I told Sarah that 97% of divorces in New York settle before a judge hands down a decision after a trial. She realized then that the first decision that she and Matthew faced wasn't whether or not they were going to come to terms but how. She asked me to tell her more about Collaborative Divorce because she didn't know much about it. This book is similar to the discussion I had with Sarah and I hope it will be helpful to others seeking to understand more about the Collaborative process.

Perhaps you and your spouse of 20 years have sadly realized that the passion is gone from the relationship, and you want to end the marriage in a peaceful way. Or maybe you still love your spouse, but you can no longer deal with his or her financial mismanagement, rude behavior or parenting problems. Or possibly your spouse had an affair, broke the law or engaged in dangerous or repulsive behavior that drove you to end the marriage. Whether the divorce request blindsided you or you initiated it, you're probably feeling a stew of emotions. You might be angry about your spouse's behavior, confused by the situation you face, overwhelmed by the uncertainty and possibly even relieved that the tensions in your marriage have finally come to a head.

You need to reclaim control, peace of mind, and a sense of stability in your life.

Here's the reality: divorce is hard no matter what process you use. This can be especially true in New York cases involving high value estates and Type A personalities. But there are better, more humane ways of settling your differences than traditional litigation. You have options. The Collaborative Divorce process is a unique method designed to be more likely to lead to better outcomes, to preserve the assets of the marital estate and to lead to long term solutions that will leave you and your children resilient and empowered.

What comes next in your life does not have to be as expensive, painful, and hijacking as you might fear. This guide to the Collaborative Divorce in New York will explain the ins and outs of this model in clear language:

Section 1: Collaborative Divorce 101

This section will define the basics: the terms and concepts that you should know. You'll learn who is involved, how things work and what to expect in terms of timelines, your own obligations and the next steps.

Section 2: Answers to FAQs about Collaborative Divorce

Next, we will answer common questions – and correct common misperceptions – about what happens during a Collaborative Divorce and what you need to do to stay in control the whole time.

Section 3: Rebuilding Your Life from the Ground Up

Whether you were married for 4 months or 40 years, the separation will likely throw your life out of alignment. We'll address how to organize your life, manage your kids, preserve your health and wellbeing, and get the social, emotional and financial support you need.

Section 4: More Divorce Related Resources

This brief reference section offers insight and links to address divorce-related problems, concerns and opportunities.

Bonus Section – Transcript of an Interview with Katherine Miller

Katherine discusses what inspired her passion for the Collaborative Divorce process, her own divorce, and words of wisdom for those who are going through this experience.

You've endured shock and disappointment recently. It's easy to get locked into a mindset of "looking backwards" in your life to figure out what went wrong and why. However, you also want to take stock of what's true now and what you want to be true once the divorce concludes. A thoughtful, compassionate approach is possible. Please enjoy this book and take heart that you will get through this difficult time and come out even stronger for the experience.

Section 1: Collaborative Divorce 101

When most New Yorkers think of "divorce," they imagine starkly lit courtrooms, judges with their brows furrowed in serious concentration, spouses hurling accusations and counter accusations, and a whole lot of drama. You can blame reality TV and courtroom procedurals for these stereotypes. But the truth is that Collaborative Divorce is generally far more peaceful.

Collaborative Divorce, at its core, is a kind of Alternative Dispute Resolution (ADR) process that allows couples to end a marriage without resorting to litigation. (Another well-known Alternative Dispute Resolution process is *mediation*: we'll cover the differences between these approaches later in this book.)

Here's the basic idea. You, your spouse, your attorney and your spouse's attorney work together to work though conflicts and hammer out agreements. In addition, you have the opportunity to work with a Collaborative Divorce coach, child specialist and financial professional in order to get the support you need to make thoughtful decisions that will help you set your life back on track. Everyone involved goes "all in" to negotiate these terms; critically, *everyone agrees in advance not to go to litigation.* All participants sign a document called a "Participation Agreement," which says that, if you fail to reach a settlement, your attorneys will withdraw from the process -- that is, they will not help you with litigation.

Since your attorneys have skin in the game, they have incentive to work towards a settlement. This Participation Agreement details the nuts and bolts of the process. For instance:

- You and your spouse will use what's known as "interest based" negotiation to focus on what matters most to you, as opposed to more adversarial types of strategic negotiation;

- You are encouraged to use the services of neutral experts to inform discussion and resolve issues;

- You will utilize fair and constructive techniques to minimize harm and emotional trauma for you and for your children;

- The Participation Agreement outlines how the communications process will work and temporarily freezes the "status quo" with respect to marital assets, insurance, real estate, etcetera, so that neither spouse can make a unilateral move absent the consent of the other person.

The main watchword is *engagement*. You, your spouse and your Collaborative professionals will meet and explore issues in a creative fashion. The focus is on building solutions, "expanding the pie" rather than simply dividing it, and on retaining dignity instead of victory, revenge and imperial notions of justice. The professional Collaborative team supports the couple in fostering more effective conflict conversations so that they are better able to openly communicate what is important to them both and find appropriate solutions.

An Appealing Approach, in Theory, But Is It Safe and Effective?

It probably sounds appealing to settle debates about who should get what, how child care arrangement will work and so forth in a civilized manner. On the other hand, you might worry that this approach sounds too "New Age-y," and that, by trusting in this approach, you will leave yourself vulnerable to an unscrupulous spouse (or attorney).

This "nice guys (and gals) finish last" fear is common and understandable. But statistics sharply rebut it. A safer, more sensitive divorce process protects children, minimizes harm and trauma, moves at an appropriate speed, often decreases legal costs and preserves more of the marital estate. It also offers intangible benefits: when you're focused on finding respectful solutions to meet needs, you tend to develop more creative ideas and harbor fewer grudges and resentments.

Collaborative Divorce is not for everyone, however, and it's not appropriate in every situation.

Fundamentally, it helps to have trust and confidence in your spouse as a negotiating partner. (Game theorists might say it has something in common with the famous 'prisoner's dilemma' puzzle.) However, even if your spouse hasn't exactly been a poster child for kindness and integrity, you can still succeed with Collaborative. In some sense, it's more about working towards your best self, as opposed to indulging in your worst fears. The process, in other words, is flexible and strong enough to handle rocky relationships and some degree of mistrust. Let's face it, most people getting divorced do not have the highest degree of trust in each other. In most cases, the Collaborative Divorce process can still be appropriate and successful.

A Brief History of Collaborative Divorce

This approach is a relatively recent innovation. In 1990, a Minnesota lawyer named Stu Webb developed the model after becoming exasperated with traditional litigation's intractable focus on "win-lose" outcomes. Webb's main insight was that divorce should be considered less a legal conflict and more a relationship conflict with legal elements. Another lawyer active during that era, Curtis J. Romanowski, independently developed a similar philosophy called "Collaborative Dispute Resolution (CDR)."

These two attorneys and other early adopters developed a set of principles for the Collaborative model, which included the following:

- Separation is primarily a personal issue, as opposed to a legal one;

- In an ideal situation, all participants should feel like they have been heard in the process, and their concerns have been addressed by the process and the result;

- Couples should spend their money on healing not fighting and they should endure less trauma;

- Children should emerge from the process with fewer scars;

- Attorneys should enjoy their work more and feel more fundamentally fulfilled by it.

A key insight that sparked the popularity of this model was the idea that the attorneys would agree to abandon cases that they couldn't settle, rather than shift to litigation.

Since its founding, the Collaborative model has spread throughout the U.S., Canada, and beyond; if trends hold, the approach will become increasingly mainstream over the next decade, potentially overtaking traditional approaches.

Collaborative Divorce is similar in intent to another Alternative Dispute Resolution approach called *mediation* but can be distinguished by a number of salient features. Like the Collaborative model, mediation also takes place out of the courtroom. A neutral third party, known as a mediator, helps the parties try to come to agreements. Mediation can also help couples avoid costly, drawn out courtroom battles and the two processes can be quite different.

Two Ways of Negotiating During Collaborative

During traditional negotiations, most people default to what's known as **"position-based" bargaining**. Prior to meeting or early during the discussions, each side stakes a position -- a portfolio of demands -- and then pursues that position. The negotiations then become all about obtaining these goals and seeking to deny the other party success. It's competitive and adversarial.

An arguably more compassionate approach is **"interest-based" bargaining**. First, you identify what is important to each person, and then you strive to meet those interests.

Let's say your soon-to-be ex wants the house badly. In a position-based framework, you may get nowhere fast. Even if you don't care about the house, your attorney may press you to pretend to want it in order to put pressure on the person that does. If you really do want the house (because you probably can't divide it into two parts and each live in half of it) then you work toward compromise with a common result that everyone is unhappy.

In an interest-based framework, more interesting things can happen. For instance, maybe there are different ways the underlying concerns can be met. For instance, if the spouse wants the home because he or she needs to commute easily to work, you can brainstorm alternative options (e.g. telecommuting, using a car service, finding another home or apartment near work, etc.)

The point is that interest-based discussions tend to lead to more creativity and flexibility. Both parties are motivated to try to solve each other's problems because they realize that is the best way to get what they both need.

Initiating a Collaborative Divorce

The first step is deciding that you want to go the Collaborative route. First, you will need to discuss this possibility with your spouse. Collaborative Divorce is a voluntary process that both spouses must elect.

In the transcribed interview in the bonus section of this book, there is a description of some do's and don'ts when it comes to choosing Collaborative and working through each step of the process. The Collaborative attorney will review your options, look for potential barriers or problems (e.g. signs that domestic violence has occurred or that the other spouse has mental health issues). Then you will sign a retainer and get a copy of the Participation Agreement to review. Prior to your first meeting, your attorney and your spouse's attorney will share information with each other about the major issues in the divorce as well as dynamics that need to be addressed in order to minimize surprises.

6 Hallmarks of the Collaborative Process

1. Children should be protected.

Children will not be in the room with you and your attorneys. Keep them out of substantial conversations about the divorce as much as possible. This might be obvious if they are young, and it also applies to older and even adult children.

2. Collaboratively trained experts from relevant fields help solve problems.

Collaborative Divorce is an interdisciplinary process where you work with Collaboratively trained Mental Health professionals and Financial professionals as part of a team to solve core issues that arise. Both parties agree to share the expenses of hiring these experts.

3. The process is deliberatively non-adversarial.

Collaborative does not mean that everyone is happy-go-lucky and smiling all the time. It is hard work to achieve the goal to serve everyone's needs, not to punish, get revenge, create drama or play games. This is one of the reasons why Collaborative is not for everyone. If you cannot trust your spouse to participate in an above board, respectful manner -- or if there are abuse or mental health issues at play -- another divorce process may be more appropriate.

4. The goal is an outcome that tends to be much more in tune with the fundamental needs and concerns of both parties.

Experts often describe negotiations in terms of game-theory, using jargon such as **"Lose-lose"** (both parties do not get what they want); **"Win-lose"** (one party gets satisfied, the other one does not); and **"Win-win"** (both parties walk away satisfied). This framing, however, oversimplifies what actually goes on during divorce, since human emotions – and the transformations that occur during major life transitions – are obviously complex and hard to pigeonhole.

In traditional divorce frameworks, it's true that win-lose resolutions happen more frequently, as do lose-lose outcomes. As a matter of fact, when a family ends up in the courtroom that is always a lose-lose for everyone involved. For instance, a bitter *War of the Roses*-style litigation battle can drain the couple's assets and lead to bitterness and hard feelings that linger for years, and it goes almost without saying how difficult that is for the children.

Collaborative fundamentally rejects this framing and seeks ways for both parties to meet their needs and come away feeling, if not "great" about the divorce, then at least satisfied that the process was fair and compassionate. Achieving such an outcome often takes creativity and ingenuity. For instance, let's say that a couple is haggling over who should keep the fine china that the husband's mom gave them for their wedding.

The husband wants all the china. The wife wants to split the dishes evenly. In a traditional negotiation framework, someone (or maybe both people) will have to lose. Maybe the husband will have to surrender and give up half the dishes. Maybe the wife will "capitulate" and let him have everything. Maybe they'll get so angry about the "dish-agreement" (so to speak) that they'll end up throwing the dishes at each other in a major fight that leaves them with nothing but a large pile of china shards and a wrecked dining room.

A Collaborative framework tees up different possible outcomes. The process permits the professionals to help the people go under the surface and figure out what's driving these demands. Maybe the husband wants the china because his mom recently passed away, so there are sentimental feelings at play. And maybe the wife just fears that she won't get an equitable share of the assets, since she has an inner mental script that her husband always shortchanges her and puts her second.

At the core of the disagreement are very human needs: a need for connection with the past (the husband) and a need for appreciation (the wife). By surfacing and dealing with these concerns, the Collaborative process can generate novel solutions:

- Maybe the husband keeps the dishes, but the wife gets more of some other key assets.

- Maybe the husband recognizes that his sentimental attachment to the dishes isn't something that should hold negotiations at bay, and he agrees to split up the dishes.

- Maybe they decide to give the dishes to a charity or to their kids.

If the husband realizes his mother can't be brought back by keeping the dishes, is that a "win" for him? It's not. However, his realization could be transformative for him, and that in and of itself may be helpful in his mourning process both for his mother and, perhaps, the end of the marriage.

The broader point is that the "invent more options" approach helps distinguish Collaborative from the "slice up the pie" approach of traditional methods.

5. Parties agree to full document disclosure.

The goal is to keep the process transparent, fair and streamlined. So, both parties need to disclose information to each other. You both want and need to get everything out on the table for the process to work. Frankly, this step alone is a huge cost saver.

6. A main goal is to come to an agreement that works for everyone and avoid litigation.

Collaborative is all about coming to an agreement based on what is important to the people involved and staying out of court. We take that commitment seriously. So seriously, that if the Collaborative attorneys working with the couple can't iron things out in this framework, both attorneys must withdraw; and they cannot represent either of you in a litigation.

What Does Your Lawyer Do During This Process?

The Collaborative attorney's role is rich, dynamic and multifaceted.

He or she wears many hats and serves as a coach, manager, educator, advocate and resource (the other Collaborative professionals help with these roles as well). The Collaborative attorney will advise you about your case, guide you towards creative solutions, and ensure a respectful and compassionate dialogue. Your attorney will help you organize what you need to disclose, analyze choices, and find and work effectively with your expert team. Look for someone who has an empathetic demeanor, a background in conflict resolution and a strong command of New York divorce law.

8 Advantages to Collaborative

1. You enjoy **enhanced control** over the process. Instead of letting a stranger in a black robe make decisions for you, you and your spouse can work out an arrangement autonomously with the help of the Collaborative professionals.

2. The approach leads to **less stress, anxiety and frustration** for you and your children than traditional approaches.

3. You can **develop usable insight** into yourself and your relationships, which can support you as you rebuild your life.

4. You avoid **court-related scheduling problems**. Especially if you work hard -- and/or you have young children or medical needs -- the traditional divorce process can be quite disruptive. Collaborative lets you bypass this costly logistical encumbrance.

5. Collaborative lets you **resolve the divorce privately**. Divorce is sensitive and personal. Ideally, most people prefer not to air their grievances in public. The process is discreet.

6. The lack of formality leads to **more creativity**. Instead of getting burdened by arbitrary technical and legal requirements, parties can share their

thoughts and feelings and views on things that are most important to them and, with the help of the Collaborative professionals, create customized solutions that fit their circumstances.

7. The **interdisciplinary team's insights can have positive long-term consequences**. For instance, maybe you and your spouse never really had a grip on your finances, but the financial advisor can help you develop a working budget and money management plan. Or maybe the parenting expert could help find a good therapist to address your daughter's persistent behavioral problem that she's been having at school and thus reduce stress for everyone involved.

8. In general, it **costs less than litigation** and the return on investment is much greater.

An Emotionally Intelligent Divorce

Intense emotional conflict often fuels the problems that lead to divorce and divorce itself challenges even the most emotionally even-keeled people because it touches the most sensitive areas of their lives. Yet trying to push emotions aside and remain strictly logical is not the answer. Emotions, surprisingly, can be useful in a Collaborative Divorce. The trick is for both people to use emotional intelligence to handle the issues that divorce raises.

Daniel Shapiro, the founder and head of the Harvard

International Negotiation Project, says that feelings drive people towards conflict, but they can also drive them towards resolution. Whether the conflict is between countries, he says, or between divorcing spouses, a small shift can make all the difference in moving a situation from a conflict where anger, fear, and hurt push both sides to stubbornly hold onto their opposing positions, to a situation where they can manage their differences effectively. "Shift the relational stance so it's no longer 'me versus you' but the two of us working side by side facing a shared problem," Shapiro says, and that will create a shift from emotions of stubbornness to emotions of curiosity, commitment, and maybe even compassion. Then, progress becomes possible.

In addition to creating opportunities to more effectively manage differences, using emotional intelligence brings other benefits to the divorce process --

- Emotionally intelligent parents can be more emotionally available to their children to continue to meet the kids' day-to-day needs, while also finding ways to help buffer the children from some of the stresses of the divorce.

- Emotionally intelligent parents also are good role models for their kids, setting examples of how to handle difficult situations.

- Emotional intelligence can help divorcing spouses process, rather than repress, the end of the marriage. Giving themselves permission to grieve allows natural healing to take place.

• Cultivating emotional intelligence puts divorcing spouses in the best position to start their new post-divorce lives without being paralyzed by overwhelming feelings of regret, anger, or self-recrimination.

Emotional intelligence is a skill that can be learned and cultivated. In an emotionally difficult situation like divorce, the payoff for the effort can be enormous.

Mediation: Another Sensitive Approach to New York Divorce

Like Collaborative Divorce, mediation offers an alternative, private way to separate and avoid litigation. A neutral party– the mediator--will work through the process with you. The mediator is not a judge – and thus cannot make decisions for you – but he or she can facilitate discussions leading to resolution of conflict and issues. Done right, it can be a quite empowering process.

Here's how mediation works. The couples meet together in sessions during which the mediator helps them identify the issues that need to be resolved, talk through what is most important to each of them and generate options to solve the problems they face.

Like Collaborative, mediation has multiple advantages:

• Enhanced communication (compared to litigation).

- Aims to find creative solutions to problems like how to split up the marital assets and debts.

- Costs less than litigation, because you don't have to pay for formal discovery, a court hearing or trial preparation.

- The time frame is based on the needs of the family as opposed to the court's schedule.

- The process is confidential.

- A more relaxed atmosphere that's hospitable to creativity and cooperation.

- Like Collaborative, the mediation framework lets you make decisions without the intrusion of a judge.

- Your team and your attorneys are invested in a solid, equitable outcome; in litigation, by contrast, the judge may not particularly care about the outcome and may just want to clear his or her calendar.

Selecting Your Divorce Process

If you are facing or considering divorce, you're likely right now contending with powerful emotions that flicker in intensity. One minute you might feel furious. The next minute, you might feel depressed. You might then go a few hours or days feeling neutral or numb (or relieved and then angry and then confused). It's totally normal to have strong but vacillating emotions. The key is to pause and reflect mindfully before you choose a divorce process.

Avoid making decisions about your divorce impulsively. For instance, you may be so angry (perhaps your spouse cheated on you or blindsided you by saying that he "fell out of love") that you might want to leap to litigation to punish the other person and exact maximum vengeance.

Avoid metaphorically cutting off your nose to spite your face. Impetuous actions can exact costly and far ranging consequences. Here are some factors to weigh:

1. **How much will the divorce cost, and how long will it take?**

Litigation tends to consume more money and time than either mediation or Collaborative. If you can work together as adults with the help of appropriate professionals, you will likely save both money and time.

2. **How important is privacy to you?**

Both Collaborative and mediation can keep the process closed off to the public. In litigation, any court proceedings are open to the public. It's amazing who you see in the divorce part of the courthouse.

3. **What professional support do you need and why?**

Would it be resourceful for you to work with people like a coach, a financial advisor, a parenting expert … or not? Divorce is the untangling of a complex relationship. There are many aspects to the process—external and internal.

What kind of support does your family need to transition as smoothly as possible?

4. **What do you want to feel, during the divorce and afterwards?**

Litigation might be analogous to the game of chess, where you are constantly trying to crush or checkmate the other side, and you strategize and engage in tactics to that end. Chess, particularly at the tournament level, can be quite a blood sport. Using Collaborative or mediation, meanwhile, is more like putting together a puzzle. You both work towards the same end. The more of the "puzzle" you complete, the closer you are to resolving lingering issues from the marriage.

Mediation vs. Collaboration: Which Approach Is Better?

In some situations, Collaborative makes more sense. In other situations, mediation does.

Scenarios in which opting for Collaborative probably makes more sense:

- **You want to work closely with an attorney**. For instance, maybe you just want someone in your corner the whole time; or maybe the case involves complex financial or child related issues that you would like help managing.

- **There have been power imbalances in your relationship**. For instance, maybe you worry that your spouse will dominate the proceedings and you won't get to speak your mind or address issues that are important to you.

- **You want a more structured process where the support is "baked in".** The Collaborative process is designed to be a more structured process than mediation. The lawyers will help move the process alone and you will likely receive guidance in and outside the joint sessions than you will in mediation.

Scenarios in which opting for mediation probably makes more sense:

- **You want an informal process.** In Collaborative, the interdisciplinary team must follow certain protocols and rules to keep the process orderly. Mediation can be more flexible; at its sparest, it only requires three people -- you, the mediator and your spouse.

- **You want the process to be easy to coordinate and schedule.** Logistically, it's easier to sync up schedules with a few parties than it is to coordinate an entire Collaborative team.

- **You want maximum privacy.** Confidentiality laws protect what goes on during mediation. Collaboration is also a private process, but the joint conversational sessions feel less absolutely private because there are more people in the room.

Before You Initiate the Divorce Process: Some Insights to Consider

The conventional thinking is that divorce is like a high stakes chess game or a military battle. *How can you get more or pay less? How can you maximize your assets? What can you do to undermine or counter your soon-to-be-ex's strategies? Should you "strike first"? Etc.*

Especially if your spouse betrayed you, you may be inclined to engage in this aggressive, chess-like warfare. But divorce is not a "business decision," nor is it a war or a game. A divorce touches on diverse facets (e.g. your children, your emotional life, your career, your relationships, etc.). A single-minded, muscular strategy is probably not the answer.

If you're reading this book, it is likely that your marriage or the marriage of someone you care about faces major problems; or you and your spouse may have already separated. Discuss your situation with trusted advisors, like a therapist or divorce lawyer, and get several opinions, so you can access diverse insight. Try to anticipate what you think your spouse might do when you announce your desire to get divorced. If you worry, for instance, that he or she will react in an aggressive or dangerous manner, get advice as to how best to protect yourself.
Collect relevant information and strive to be your best self. Develop your support network and think about your future.

Section 2: Answers to FAQs about Collaborative Divorce

How is property divided up during a New York divorce?

New York law considers your marriage to be a "financial partnership" Among other things, once you get married, all compensation you receive in exchange for your own efforts is marital. It's easy to unintentionally create a marital asset from a separate asset when you comingle the two. There are ways to keep finances silo-ed during a marriage -- through use of legal tools like a prenuptial agreement -- but you might be surprised by the degree to which your and your spouse's finances have been mixed. For instance, maybe you make contributions to a 401 (k) retirement plan through your work. The plan is in your name, and only you contribute to it. But the asset belongs to the marriage, which means your spouse may have a claim to some of what's in it. Whatever divorce process you choose, you will have to work out a way to equitably divide all the marital property, such as retirement accounts, pensions, stocks, homes and real estate holdings, businesses that you own, etc.

What is the difference between "equal" distribution and "equitable" distribution?

In some cases, it is possible to split assets (or debts) right down the middle. But when you're dealing with sentimental objects or items like jewelry, works of art, cars, and furniture, you often can't just split them down the middle.

Part of the process of getting divorced is finding a way to equitably divide assets and debts. This is one of the areas in which the Collaborative process really shines. For instance, maybe both of you want the dog. Obviously, you cannot "split" a dog; however, you can negotiate a creative arrangement. For instance, maybe the dog travels with the children or lives primarily with one person but spends two weekends a month with the other. It might even make sense for one person to give up the dog altogether in exchange for something else that is very significant for that person. The opportunity to really think through what each person wants and why is one of the hallmarks of the Collaborative process.

How can you create a caring and thoughtful parenting time schedule?

Discussions about sharing your children's time can become fraught and emotional. Again, this is an arena in which the Collaborative process can be useful. There are very likely many mutually acceptable solutions to your parenting dilemmas, especially if both parents are loving towards their kids.

This parenting plan must be able to accommodate contingencies. For instance, what if you or your ex-spouse moves out of state or moves to a remote location in New York? Where will the children go to school? How will the transitions work? What if your work schedules change or if you need to go out of town? How should the plan be amended if and when new significant others enter the picture? What if the child has a disability, an emotional problem, special medical needs, or a suddenly demanding athletic schedule? What general process can you use to resolve disputes, so that you are not constantly bumping heads?

There is no plug-and-play formula, but the Collaborative approach can help you work out the right solutions, so you are not left trying to figure out how to make these decisions on your own. The open nature of the Collaborative framework will also help think through (and iron out) the wrinkles of time sharing.

How does "alimony" work in New York?

Alimony -- known as "spousal support" or "maintenance" in New York -- involves one former spouse providing financial support to the other. For instance, perhaps you have been the primary breadwinner. Your spouse may request ongoing payments, at least until he can get back on his feet and reboot his career. Maintenance payments could be "rehabilitative" meaning for a limited duration in order to permit the recipient to get to a place where he is self-supporting. Permanent maintenance is unusual in New York, and it can last much longer, potentially for the rest of your life or your spouse's life.

Maintenance has been a tax deduction for payors for many years (and includable in the recipient's taxable income), however, the tax laws passed in late 2017 limit the deductibility of maintenance to people who sign their settlement agreement or are divorced prior to December 31, 2018.

What can influence spousal maintenance amounts?

New York Law on maintenance is in a state of uncertainty at the time of this writing. In 2015, the New York State legislature passed a statute instituting a formula for people earning up to $175,000 (that amount increases every other year by the inflation rate and is currently $183,000). This statute only applies to cases that were started after January 23, 2016.

The formula when the payor is also paying child support is:

    a. subtract 25% of the maintenance payee's income from 20% of the maintenance payor's income;

    b. multiply the sum of the maintenance payor's income and the maintenance payee's income by 40% and subtract the maintenance payee's income from the result;

    c. the lower of the two amounts will be the guideline amount of maintenance.

The formula when the payor is NOT also paying child support is:

    a. 25% of the maintenance payee's income from 30% of the maintenance payor's income;

b.   multiply the sum of the maintenance payor's income and the maintenance payee's income by 40% and subtract the maintenance payee's income from the result;

c.   the lower of the two amounts will be the guideline amount of maintenance.

If the formula results in a number that is less than zero, then there will be no maintenance.

If a payor earns over the cap amount (currently $183,000), then the court must first perform the calculation on the income up to the cap and then, for income exceeding the cap, any additional maintenance is at the discretion of the court. The decision of the court MUST consider 15 factors in deciding how much maintenance should be awarded. These factors are similar to factors people consider but may have a different emphasis or priority. Here are some examples:

- The financial circumstances of both spouses, including your and your spouse's income history, assets, debts, education and career trajectory.

- The length of the marriage.

- The age and health of both parties.

- The need to pay for exceptional additional expenses for the child/children, including but not limited to, schooling, day care and medical treatment.

How long will maintenance last?

The 2015 statute also set out advisory guidelines for judges on how long maintenance should last. Those guidelines are advisory only and, at the time of this writing, we do not know how strictly the courts will interpret them. Here they are

Length of Marriage	Duration of Maintenance
0-15 years	15% to 30%
15-20 years	30% to 40%
Over 20 years	35% to 50%

Once we figure out what the cash flow between the ex-spouses will be and whether or not there will be maintenance paid from one to the other, we then need to plan for how it may change over time or in event of certain contingencies other than the passage of time. For example:

- Relationship changes. Will there change in the support payments if the recipient gets remarried or moves in with someone new?

- Career changes. If the supported spouse gets a huge raise or promotion (or, conversely, the supporting spouse gets fired or demoted), the maintenance amount can potentially be changed. It is not easy to renegotiate in the moment and so we try to foresee these contingencies and discuss them as part of the Collaborative process.

What factors help determine a child support award in New York?

Child support is comprised of two parts: First, there's the basic child support obligation, which is intended to cover expenses like food, shelter and clothing for the child or children.

Basic child support is paid from one parent to the other to help support the child or children in the recipient's home. The New York Child Support Guideline statutes calculate this "basic" child support as a percentage. The Child Support formula is similar to the maintenance formula in that it has a percentage applied to the combined parental income up to a cap (at the time of publication of this book, the cap is $143,000) but the court has discretion to apply the formula to the entire parental income if the circumstances so warrant. The percentages are:
- One child: 17%
- Two children: 25%
- Three children: 29%
- Four children: 31%
- Five children: no less than 35%

The formulas apply to the parents before tax income with only certain limited deductions permitted. The maintenance paid by one spouse to the other is deducted from the maintenance payor's income for the purposes of the child support calculation and added to the recipient's income.

Then, there are the "add-on" categories in addition to the "basic" the child support award, which include child care, health care and educational expenses. These add-on expenses are often paid to a third party such as a doctor, babysitter or tutor.

New York Law does give parents the right to opt out of the statutory formula and choose a different structure for certain reasons that must be clearly articulated, as long as particular criteria are met.

Child support is not deductible to the payor, nor taxable income to the recipient.

Can child support be modified over time?

Parents may seek a modification or change of a child support order based upon a showing of:

- A substantial change in circumstances;
- The passage of three years since the order was issued, (this only applies to agreements or orders made on or after October 13, 2010); or
- A 15% increase or decrease in either parent's income since the original order was issued (this only applies to agreements or orders made on or after October 13, 2010).

Substantial Change in Circumstances

What exactly constitutes a "substantial change of circumstances" varies from case to case. Some examples include changes in a child's needs, a paying parent's illness or significant involuntary decrease in that parent's income.

Three Years Have Passed

A parent can file a petition for the court to recalculate a child support order every three years in situations where either parent's income has changed. It is important to note that the ability to file a petition is by no means a guarantee that a change will be granted.

Change in Income by 15%

If a paying parent's income decreases by at least 15%, he/she can file a petition for "downward modification," or a reduction to child support. Parents petitioning a court for a downward modification because of a decrease in income must be able to show the court that the reduced income was not voluntary and that they engaged in real efforts to secure more income or other employment.

If the paying parent's income has increased, the receiving parent may petition the court for an "upward modification" or increase to the previous child support order.

It is important to know that none of the above circumstances create an automatic change nor to they allow a parent to change the child support being paid without the written and acknowledged consent of both parents or a court order.

What is "legal separation"? How is it distinct from marriage and divorce? What happens during it?

Legal separation exists as kind of twilight between marriage and divorce. Divorce puts an end to your marriage; legal separation does not. The Collaborative process also applies to people seeking a legal separation either as a stop on the road to divorce or as an end in and of itself.

A legal separation could mean you live as all-but-divorced with separate finances, a formal separation agreement and completely separate lives. It could also mean something less formal. In order to be legally separated, however, you need a formal separation agreement or a court judgment. Some couples who want to avoid divorce -- for religious or personal reasons -- get a legal separation as a stop gap solution. Sometimes people decide to stay legally separated for a period of time in order to allow one person to remain on the other's health insurance plan.

What are the Unique Features of High Net Worth New York Divorces?

New York has what are known as *equitable distribution laws* for marital property.

As we discussed before, this doesn't necessarily mean that everything is split 50-50. In high net worth divorces, the marital estate is often large, complex and sprawling. A business (or businesses) owned by the couple may need to be valuated and split up or sold off. Hidden assets and hidden debts may need to be unearthed and discussed. The tax implications can be profound, as can the inheritance issues.

With greater – and more diverse – assets come more complex discussions. High net worth divorces sometimes take a bit longer to sort through and require some financial sophistication and wise guidance. Done wrong, such divorces can lead to the needless hemorrhaging of assets, high taxes, and hurt feelings. The couple also needs to be especially aware of possible fraud and theft. For instance, unscrupulous "friends" of the family (or outright thieves) may try to take advantage of the couple's emotionally vulnerable state to tap their assets.

High net worth divorce can also have implications that go beyond the immediate family. For instance, if the couple owns a business together, that business (and its employees, stakeholders, customers, etcetera) can all be affected. For an extreme example, consider the 2014 divorce between Harold and Sue Ann Hamm. Mr. Hamm founded and owned a company called Continental Resources, valued at its peak at nearly $20 billion. Its enormous size and scope made it as economically powerful as small nation! Mrs. Hamm ended up with an award worth nearly $1 billion -- and she later appealed that decision.

Continental Resources' employees and vendors watched the proceeds with bated breath. The judge's decision could have effectively destroyed the company. Residents throughout North Dakota, where Continental Resources does a lot of business, watched also, because the outcome had such big implications for the lives and livelihoods of everyone in the state.

What effects will divorce have on your children, and what can you do to protect them and nurture them through the process?

What can be done to protect children whose parents are divorcing? There are two separate, but related tactics parents can take to protect their children while they are in the process of divorce.

1. Parents can effectively deal with their own emotional fallout from the divorce.

I do not think that it is possible to separate what some people call the "emotional divorce" from the legal divorce. My experience is that emotions influence thinking and that the best way to prevent emotions from taking over is to get help to process the emotional impact of the divorce.

Everyone has an emotional response to divorce. Even the partner who chooses to end the marriage has feelings that come up around that decision and its repercussions for the family. Dealing with what comes up emotionally will help parents to protect their children from their own anger, sadness or other reaction to the divorce -- both the end of the marriage and the resolution process.

2. Parents can separate the resolution of the parenting plan from the financial negotiation.

Of course, the entire settlement or resolution of a divorce must all work together, and any parenting plan must be financially supported by the rest of the settlement. Yet, if the parents can make explicit their intention to support the parenting plan they choose -- actually setting forth a written parenting plan that involves both parents in the lives of the children as frequently and thoroughly as possible -- this strategy is likely to result in a plan that truly puts the children first.

Neither of the above guidelines is easy to do, and they work independently of each other—although working through your own emotional fallout does make separating the parental responsibilities from the financial details far easier. Divorce is a scary thing to go through. It is sad, expensive and incredibly disruptive for the entire family. Finding a way to protect your children will likely not be easy. From the outside, it seems like it should be. Everyone talks about protecting the children as something to which they aspire -- either as professionals or parents. In reality, it takes courage and self-honesty. Ask yourself: how would you want your children to describe you as a parent going through your divorce? That answer will set you on the right path.

Fortunately, research suggests that the majority of children of divorce go on to lead normal, healthy, emotionally adjusted lives after their parents separate. For the first three years or so after a separation, children in general do tend to show signs of distress: their performance at school may drop, for instance. But most children prove resilient.

One risk may be rapid repartnering. In his book, The Marriage-Go-Round, Johns Hopkins University sociologist, Andrew Cherlin, argues that divorcing parents may put their children at risk when they repartner too rapidly, because this behavior can create instability at home.

Sometimes, divorced parents think that children should ideally be living with two adults. As a result, many people who get divorced feel obligated –for the sake of the children–to repartner fast. Cherlin's research, however, suggests that such a strategy can backfire. It's bad for the child's development if partners continually enter and exit the family (e.g. a string of boyfriends or girlfriends come and go), because this activity can be destabilizing.

How should you talk to your children about the divorce?

Consider treating these important conversations almost like you might treat a sensitive business meeting with a new client. Take time before to think through your goals and values. Visualize a positive outcome. Figure out what language you want to use, and even practice rehearsing in private or with a friend. Contemplate what could wrong and figure out how you would best respond. For instance, let's say one of your children makes accusations or gets extremely emotional. What will you do? What will you want to avoid doing? In addition, take advantage of support systems and resources that you have, such as close friends or family members, a therapist, your divorce attorney, etc.

You might also want to reflect on important conversations afterwards. Write down on paper what happened, what mistakes you made and what progress you made. Get these concerns off your mind, so that you can focus on rebuilding your life and moving on.

How can you make Collaborative meetings more productive?

Write down your thoughts and feelings in a journal, reflecting on the sessions. Ask good questions of yourself. Is anything about the divorce process making you uncomfortable or, conversely, meeting your needs quite well? Is your attorney giving you the support you need? In an ideal world, how might the next session go? What would happen? Take time to write down your thoughts about the process. Share those thoughts and feelings with your lawyer. Together, you can devise a strategy to make the meetings better for you.

Along those lines, recognize that your thoughts and feelings about the divorce (and about your life in general, as it relates to the divorce) *will not occur in a linear fashion*. Insights will come to you at inconvenient times: at 4 o'clock in the morning, when you wake from a dream; when you're stuck in traffic; when you're in the middle of a meeting at work; and when you're checking out at the supermarket. Most people just let those thoughts go -- i.e. they don't consciously collect and process them. However, you may find it useful to write those thoughts down on a notepad or computer when you have them, so that you can act on them appropriately at a suitable time.

For instance, you may be having coffee with a friend and talking about what is going on. During that conversation, you may realize that planning for retirement is more important to you than staying in the house. Or, let's say you wake up one morning and suddenly realize that you need to go out of town over a holiday weekend and that this trip will interfere with your time-sharing arrangement. If you fail to write down this concern so you can discuss it with your spouse and/or attorney, subconsciously, a part of you will remember. **Write down your thoughts, stresses and ideas about the divorce**, so that you can think more effectively about them and spend less time and energy worrying unproductively about them.

A journal can also help you process what is coming up for you emotionally. Many people find that writing down how they are feeling helps them cope with the myriad of confusing emotions that come up for them during the divorce process. Make sure to keep your journal in a safe place though. It can be detrimental to your best interests if it falls into the wrong hands.

Solicit feedback from your attorney throughout the process. *Based on similar cases that you have handled in the past, how do you think mine is going? What could I be doing differently or better? What should our next steps be?* The more clarity you have, the better you will sleep at night, and the more you can focus on truly productive activities.

What's a concrete example of how Collaborative Divorce can solve an issue in a more productive, less "dramatic" way than litigation?

Let's say that your spouse just got offered a promising position out of town in Seattle. She's the higher earner, so whether she moves could have a major impact on the custody arrangement. However, you would prefer to remain in New York; you're living in your family's old house, which you inherited from your parents, and you'd like to keep it.

Consider two possible scenarios. In scenario one -- a litigious solution -- your ex-wife decides to go to Seattle to pursue her career advancement. In so doing, she knowingly sacrifices some custody rights, which pains her and also creates challenges for you, since you don't have enough time or money to provide the kind of child care you would like to offer. The court decision leaves everyone somewhat unhappy. You keep the house but wind up with more child care responsibilities than you'd like. Your wife gets to advance her career, but she must sacrifice significant time with the kids. Your children, meanwhile, must grow up with two parents living on two coasts; and both parents are now wrestling with guilt and frustration over the situation.

In scenario two -- a Collaborative one -- the process leads to more productive, expansive brainstorming about how to get everyone's needs met. Maybe you realize that you could reduce your expenses as well as your child care obligations by selling your home and moving to Seattle. Given your wife's new, higher salary, she can offer more financial support, and she benefits from having everyone in the same city, because the arrangement is logistically easier, and she can see her children more often. Finally, the children win because they get to grow up in one city with both parents present in their lives.

Does the Collaborative process lead to better long-term cooperation and success?

Although researchers haven't conducted any definitive scientific trials, anecdotal evidence certain supports the value of Collaborative and surveys conducted by the International Academy of Collaborative Professionals confirm this impression. Many people think of divorce as a zero sum game in which victory is defined in terms of how many concessions you can win:

- The more marital assets you retain, the better.

- The more control you have over your children, the better.

- The more you can punish a spouse who hurt you, the better.

These intuitions are actually off base, when you dig into the research and also have the opportunity to observe what happens to couples going through this process. A more thoughtful divorce process – even one that yields close to the same tangible results as a contentious process – will likely lead to better feelings about the marriage, the divorce and also more satisfaction with the outcome.

Additional anecdotal evidence suggests that when stakeholders in negotiations tend to adhere to agreements when they make them on a voluntary basis as opposed to when someone imposes the rules on them. Do you want your wife to abide by a timesharing plan? Do you want easy transitions when you drop off the kids every week? When you and your spouse work together to iron out your arrangement -- as opposed to having the court forcing something on you -- odds are that you'll both be more likely to take ownership for that arrangement and respect it.

What are some red flags that suggest that a Collaborative approach may not be possible?

- **Abuse or neglect.**

Has your spouse been physically, emotionally or verbally abusive to you and your children? Collaborative is probably not appropriate.

- **Refusal to participate.**

For instance, maybe she misses three sessions in a row or keeps rejecting candidate experts without really giving good reasons. Your attorney should be alert for these signs and help you figure out what actions you can take, if any, to reboot the process.

- **Persistent Dishonesty.**

Has your partner engaged in duplicitous or unethical behavior, such as consistent lying or hiding money? If so, Collaborative may not be appropriate. You need a baseline of trust for the process to work right. If you have questions about what level of trust is required, you should ask a Collaborative attorney for guidance.

What are some good ways to prepare for negotiations?

It's important to do some soul searching about what is really important to you and it can be very useful to get some help with this task. You attorney or a divorce coach can help you think about not only where you are but also where you want to go. Divorce sits at the interchange between where you have been and where you are going. If you think only about where you've been, it will be hard to set yourself on a road toward where you want to go. This isn't to say that you will get everything you want -- that probably won't happen. However, it can be very helpful to acknowledge and emphasize what factors are most important to you.

Another powerful concept that's useful in any negotiation: the BATNA.

Authors Roger Fisher and William Ury defined it this way: "The reason you negotiate is to produce something better than the results you can obtain without negotiating. What are those results? What is that alternative? What is your BATNA -- your Best Alternative To a Negotiated Agreement? That is the standard against which any proposed agreement should be measured."

Developing a Best Alternative to a Negotiated Agreement can be a complex process. You need to think through contingencies and plan. But it can offer practical benefits.

For instance, let's say you're discussing with your spouse what to do about custody of the dog. You realize in advance that having the dog live with you is not that important to you. You wouldn't be willing to end the Collaborative process and go to litigation over the pet sharing. Your BATNA in that case might be to just let him have the dog and buy another pet.

In other cases, however, your limits might be stronger. For instance, if your spouse keeps moving the goalpost of what he wants and there doesn't seem like there is any way to meet his needs, your BATNA might be to end the Collaborative process and go to litigation, because getting through the divorce is important to you.

What else can you do to make the Collaborative sessions more productive and more likely to succeed?

Come to the sessions rested, fed, well dressed and prepared. You might also want to schedule a rewarding activity afterwards, such as an afternoon at the salon or a meal with a friend. Also, visualize how you want to be during this process. Imagine what you could do or say that would be unproductive, and then define how to be in the opposite terms. For instance:

- *I'm shy: what if I fail to say what I really want during the negotiations?* Would translate to: *I am clear and articulate about what I need and want during the negotiations.*

- *What if my spouse and I get into the same arguments we always have?* Translates to: *I will allow the professional team to guide us away from the same old arguments that lead nowhere.*

- *What if I feel stressed out and overwhelmed?* Translates to: *I will come to the sessions feeling restored, alert, compassionate, and ready to do business.*

Are there any positive aspects of divorce?

Especially if you did not choose to get divorced, you might be thinking *No Way*. But consider -- if only for an exercise -- focusing on what you might be gaining instead of just what you're losing. Here are some ideas:

- *The divorce has given me an opportunity to find someone who will really care about me and love me for who I am.*

- *I have time to rebuild my life and have a second chapter that goes in a new and satisfying direction.*

- *I now have an opportunity to reinvent myself, career wise, meet new people, and go on new adventures that I otherwise might never have done.*

- *Although I didn't want the divorce, many things about the marriage and our relationship bothered me – including XYZ – and now I won't have to deal with those problems.*

Section 3: Rebuilding Your Life from the Ground Up

Whether your husband announced over the dinner table, out of the blue, that he was "no longer in love," or you've been contemplating a divorce for years, you need to prepare for diverse life transitions ahead.

Life commitments will vie for your attention before, during and after the divorce. To that end, you might benefit from exploring strategies about how to juggle your diverse workload. In this section, we'll touch on tools, strategies and philosophies of self-management to help you throughout the divorce and afterwards as well.

Get a Sense of the Landscape of Your Commitments

Divorce creates temporary uncertainty. Human beings need stability to concentrate and be effective.

Neuropsychological research has shown that short-term memory is much more limited than one might imagine. A normal human memory can only store seven bits of basic information at any one time. Add any more, and you will start to forget things. Your subconscious, however, won't forget that you need to remember something, and this will add to your anxiety.

43

The process is similar to what happens to a computer when you overtax the Random Access Memory (RAM). If you store too much in RAM, the computer will slow down, make mistakes, and lose efficiency. Likewise, when you clog up your mind with too many unfinished commitments, it's easy to become sluggish, depressed and demotivated.

Fortunately, some exercises can help you meet this challenge. Here's one approach that you might find resourceful. Cordon off three or four hours, and spend that time writing down everything that's on your mind about any commitments that you've made about anything – large or small. These can run the gamut from:

- *Get more food for the dog.*

- *Finalize the divorce.*

- *Clean up yard after storm.*

- *Hike the Appalachian Trail.*

Do a "brain dump" of everything that's on your mind about all areas of your life. You might think that your list might number in thousands of items. But most people only generate a few hundred items. You will find, perhaps to your great surprise, that just the act of writing down these things in an objective form – on paper or on the computer – will give you an immediate energy boost and stress relief.

You will see that there is actually an end to all the "stuff" that you have set out to accomplish. It's not an infinite list. In his books Getting Things Done and Making It All Work, bestselling author David Allen fleshes out more details of this organizational philosophy. Very briefly: once you go through this brain dump phase, Allen recommends that you process your commitments. Go through each one of your line items and you ask yourself two questions about them:

1. **What am I trying to accomplish about this item?**

2. **What is the next physical step in the real world that I would take, if I focused just on handling this challenge right now?**

For instance, maybe you wrote on your list "do something about dad." When you process the list, you will have to get clear about the "something" that you want to about dad. Maybe dad's been more than usually forgetful recently; you worry that he might be developing dementia. In that case, you create a project along the lines of "resolve worries about dad and dementia." The very next step might be to call your Uncle Phil to discuss what to do next.

Just answering those two questions for every item on your list should give you an enhanced sense of control and perspective. Lingering unfinished commitments will no longer lurk in the back of your mind, and you'll free up your mental resources.

It's hard to feel good about what you do, unless you know what you're *not* doing.

The goal here is not to create a massive, scary to-do list but rather to relieve your brain of the need to be the bookkeeper of your stuff. You do not need to implement this system in its entirety to reap the benefits. But the main point is that you want some system – ideally, that's external and written down – to track the diverse issues that you face.

Taking Care of Yourself While Going Through a Divorce

Divorce can impact health and wellbeing, increasing the risk of weight gain or loss, sleeplessness, cardiac issues, depression and more. So how you can take control of your health during this tumultuous time?

Obviously, this is not a medical book; check with your doctor before changing anything about your diet, exercise or supplemental routine. But consider at least researching the following ideas:

- **Reduce the amount of <u>refined sugar and refined white flour</u> that you consume**. The "ideal" diet is obviously a subject of hot debate. But almost all standard diets, whether vegan, paleo, macrobiotic or other, restrict these nonnutritive sources of calories, especially soda and other forms of liquid sugar. Conversely, make sure to get adequate nutrition, including <u>healthy fats</u> and proteins and green vegetables.

- **Find an exercise program that works well for you**. Powerful research suggests that safe, <u>slow resistance training</u> may be useful at improving insulin sensitivity, staving off osteoporosis, and building bone density. Exercise is also a good way to relieve stress.

- **Get enough sunlight and fresh air**. Especially if you live in New York City, odds are that you spend a lot of time indoors. Obviously, you don't want to get too much sunlight and burn, but new research suggests that safe levels of sun exposure may improve vitamin D levels. Spending time outdoors can be obviously refreshing and perhaps physiologically necessary.

- **Get enough rest**. This is easier said than done, particularly if you face anxiety because of the divorce. Consider avoiding using your computer, your TV, your phone and other glowing rectangles hours before bed, so that your natural circadian rhythms and melatonin levels can help with the sleep process, and try to practice getting up at the same time every day.

- **Find and cultivate social support.** Now is absolutely the time to reach out to friends, family members and others who will lift you up spiritually and support you. Be choosy about the people you allow to influence your life. Some studies suggest that the five people around us most often have a profound influence on our personalities and our dispositions towards the world. Choose your close confidants well.

- **Along those lines, it may be best to avoid diving too deeply into any new relationships**. Doing so could be destabilizing; it could also make the divorce process harder. Clean up after the divorce, and get your life organized first. There will be time to date and possibly repartner, but one thing at a time!

- **Step outside of your comfort zone and ask for help**. Do you need assistance with child care, a shoulder to cry on, or just a few meals delivered to your house so that you don't have to slave over a stove? Don't be shy. Ask for help!

- **Consider <u>engaging in introspection</u>, such as meditation, yoga or prayer**. Some research suggests that people who engage in regular mindful mediation practice (15 to 45 minutes a day) enjoy benefits ranging from reduced stress to better health markers to more empathy and concentration. Research also suggests that meditation might actually be able boost to boost what's known as the "hedonic set point" – your baseline level of happiness. In any event: something to consider.

Taking Back Control of Your Finances and Career After a Divorce

Divorce can undermine your finances in ways that are both quite obvious and not so obvious. For instance, your tax filing status will change. So how can you get handle on what the future will hold for you regarding your finances, living expenses, career, and so forth?

It is important to place the divorce in the context of the rest of your life. What will the future hold and what do you need to do to plan for it? Work with a financial advisor to get your fundamentals in order or to follow up on the work done by the Collaborative financial neutral. Ask and answer the following critical questions to shed light on your possible next steps:

- Have you made a budget for yourself now that you're single, or do you understand the budget created in the Collaborative process?

- How much information do you currently have about your financial situation?

- What are your long-term financial goals?

- What are you doing to make those goals a reality? Do you need a referral to an appropriate financial advisor?

- How are you tracking those projects?

- Whom do you have in your corner to get this work done?

- How will your career goals and trajectory need to change in light of the divorce?

Maybe the divorce will lead to a profound shift regarding how you think about yourself, your career, your skill sets and what you want to do in the world. Or maybe you had been a stay at home parent or trailing spouse; you need a new path just out of financial necessity.

In his book, Ready for Anything, David Allen offers the following instructive analogy:

"Ever had the feeling that you just woke up on a soccer field, being run over by bigger, meaner, uglier, and faster players, and you haven't the vaguest idea what you're doing there? You find yourself beaten, bloody, and muddy – and things seem to be getting worse!

To get a grip, what must you do? First, you have to accept what the game is and know where your goal is. When you can see your target and identify with getting there, you quickly lose interest in how beaten, bloody or muddy you are. Now you're into the challenge! But even if you know where you're headed, you will still feel paralyzed and at the mercy of forces larger than yourself, until you do one thing: determine the next move...

Success in life may have more to do with how fast you can accept and get started on the new game than with how good you got at playing any of the old ones."

The divorce has, effectively, knocked you down and changed the playing field. So, what are your new goals, and what are you going to do about them? Your Collaborative attorney can be an invaluable resource in terms of helping you find the support you need to make the transition out of divorce and into a successful post divorce life.

Get clear about how much money you have in the bank; what your assets and debts are; and what's happening with your current job or career. Then get clear about where you want to go. This requires some imagination. Allow yourself to dream big. Then connect the dots.

For instance, let's say that you've been out of work for the past eight years raising two kids. You have limited resources now, but you realize that you want to become a well-known business coach for women. To get from where you are to where you want to be won't happen overnight. But having clarity on your end points – where you are now, and where you want to be – can serve as a positive framework to guide your decision making.

Parenting During the Storm of a Divorce

Whether you have a tiny baby at home or three rambunctious, semiautonomous teenagers roaming the house, you need systems to parent effectively during your divorce.

A single page is way too small a space to discuss the ins and outs of this challenge – to address the possible strategies and tactics you could use. But here are a few outside resources that can help you address some of the challenges ahead:

- Four Ways to Help Your Teenage Daughter Cope With Divorce -- http://www.huffingtonpost.com/terry-gaspard-msw-licsw/4-ways-to-help-your-teena_b_3241284.html

- The Top 5 Mistakes Divorced Parents Make -- http://www.webmd.com/parenting/features/top-5-mistakes-divorced-parents-make

- Age-by-Age Guide to What Children Understand About Divorce -- http://www.parents.com/parenting/divorce/coping/what-children-understand-about-divorce/

--

- [11 Rules for Helping Your Child Deal With Divorce](http://www.parents.com/parenting/divorce/coping/helping-child-deal-with-divorce/) -- http://www.parents.com/parenting/divorce/coping/helping-child-deal-with-divorce/

- [Dealing With Divorce: 7 Tips to Protect Your Kids](http://www.aaets.org/article115.htm) -- http://www.aaets.org/article115.htm

Just remember that you are not responsible for anyone else's feelings: Not your children's, not your spouse's, not your family's. You can only control your own habits, behaviors and emotional reactions. If your teenager screams *I hate you, mom, for divorcing dad!* You can neither deny her emotion, nor make it all better. But you *can* control how you react. Strive to do so mindfully. Forgive yourself for your trespasses -- you are going through a hard time -- and strive for as much empathy as you can access.

Be an active listener. Pay attention to what your kids are genuinely needing and feeling. For instance, if your daughter screams *I hate you, mom!* instead of saying things like *No, you don't!* or *I'm so sorry about what I've done to you!* or *You're crushing me with that remark!* consider just reflecting her experience back to her: *I get the sense that the divorce process is incredibly stressful for you right now, and you feel like you hate me.*

In other words, rather than respond with guilt or shame, reflect what you see and what you think the other person is going through. This simple process can be surprisingly healing.

Section 4: More Divorce Related Resources

- Divorce financial planning: 8 tips to get what you need in a divorce -- http://www.cbsnews.com/news/divorce-financial-planning-8-tips-to-get-what-you-need-in-a-divorce/

- Top 10 Tips for a Great Divorce -- https://www.psychologytoday.com/blog/because-im-the-mom/201101/top-10-tips-great-divorce

- 5 Tips For a Drama-Free Divorce -- http://psychcentral.com/blog/archives/2013/03/30/5-tips-for-a-drama-free-divorce/

- 22 Tips to Transform Your Financial Life After a Divorce -- http://www.dailyfinance.com/2014/07/28/22-step-divorce-financial-checklist/

- Experienced in Love and Money -- http://www.nytimes.com/2009/11/21/your-money/21money.html?pagewanted=all

- 5 Things You Need To Know About Happiness After Divorce -- http://www.huffingtonpost.com/2014/03/25/life-after-divorce_n_5029684.html

- When Mental Illness Leads To Divorce: What You Should Know -- http://www.yourtango.com/2013191101/when-mental-illness-leads-divorce-what-you-should-know

- How I Bounced Back From Divorce -- http://mariashriver.com/blog/2014/04/how-i-bounced-back-from-divorce-laine-ward/

- 6 Little-Known Benefits Of Being Divorced -- http://www.huffingtonpost.com/2013/10/26/divorce-benefits_n_4145361.html

- 5 Ways to Be More Empathetic -- http://time.com/3562863/5-ways-to-be-more-empathetic/

<u>Conclusion</u>

There's no beating around the bush: divorce is hard.

Whether you use mediation, Collaborative or a traditional process, you face stress, hard decisions and emotional challenges in the weeks and months to come. However, not all divorces are created equal. You can deploy smart tools, techniques, strategies and philosophies to approach this big life challenge in an open-hearted yet intentional way to get what you want, to preserve what you need, and to live your values as we go through the process.

We hope that this primer on Collaborative Divorce has positioned you effectively and given you some comfort and solace. If you have any questions about Collaborative or about our process, we would love to learn more about you and provide a confidential consultation. Please reach out to us at 914-738-7765 or connect with us through www.westchesterfamilylaw.com.

No matter what happens with your journey, good luck and appreciate yourself. You will make it. As Winston Churchill once famously said, "This is not the end. This is not even the beginning of the end. But it is, perhaps, the end of the beginning." Good luck!

Bonus Section: Interview with Katherine Miller

Adam: What got you excited about Collaborative law? What inspired you to get into this line of work?

Katherine: My parents, my grandmother and my former husband all worked in the field of psychology. And I went to law school because I was interested in justice and in people. It didn't take me long to realize that law school wasn't really about justice!

I was always interested in doing family law from the very beginning of my career. I grew up in Manhattan, and, ultimately, I came back to the city and started working in a family law firm in 1988. By 1990, I was already signed up to take mediation training, because I felt like there was a real disconnect between the family and the family law system. So, I took a mediation training, and I started to try to integrate those mediation techniques into my matrimonial negotiations. [My firm's] practice was about half matrimonial litigation and half child welfare litigation - a lot of litigation!

And in New York, 97% of cases settle before a judge hands down a decision after a trial. So obviously these negotiations were really mostly on the road to settlement. In every single case, I ran into the same problem ... the other lawyer. Because here I was trying to talk about what was important to the parties -- what mattered to them, how their kids were doing and all that sort of stuff -- and we couldn't seem to get on the same page about the basis of the negotiations... They [wanted to talk about] rights and obligations as opposed to needs and interests... which was really frustrating.

So then, when I got divorced myself -- and there was no Collaborative in New York back then -- my ex and I started mediation. But he was uncomfortable mediating, because he wasn't a lawyer. So, we actually ended up settling in a litigation framework, but in a very Collaborative way. We never we went to court, we settled in a conference room. But after that experience, I decided that I would rather sell shoes than to continue to practice the way that I had been in a litigation model where we often settled on "the courthouse steps"

And I actually took steps to lead a new life. I left my job and moved out of city. I got remarried. I had another baby. I did some mediation and some other work along the way. And then a friend of mine called me up and said, *you know, you should come take this Collaborative training.* And I was like, *oh come on, how could it really be any different, it's all bunch of lawyers, right?* She said *no, really, I think you'll like it.* And so, I did.

Within 15 minutes of showing up at that training, I felt like I was coming home. *This* was the way that I had always wanted to practice... with a multi-disciplinary team that works together to help people solve the problems that they have... to successfully fashion an appropriate solution for their families. And I decided, *all right, I'll give this law thing another shot.* And I started to take my own firm more seriously. I got an office, engaged in a lot of mediation and Collaborative work, and the firm has grown since then.

Adam: Fantastic. So, your passion for Collaborative Divorce came from your personal experiences as well as kind of your intellectual convictions?

Katherine: Absolutely.

Adam: And when you were going through your own divorce, did you represent yourself?

Katherine: Well, you know that old saying: *that a man who represents himself has a fool for a client.* So, I didn't represent myself. But obviously I played a big role in the negotiation. But I think it's very hard to have the same perspective as a party than as a lawyer.

Adam: Sure. In terms of your background immersed in the world of therapy... did that give you unique insight into the sort of psychology of divorce -- something other lawyers might not share?

Katherine: Well, I had no training as a therapist. I mean, I went to law school. My parents are psychologists. My ex husband is a psychologist. My grandmother was a psychologist. I grew up with that approach to the world. That said, you know, I think I have a psychologically advanced view of what people are going through. I am very sensitive to what's going on with them emotionally. And I think the brain research shows that decision-making is made in the emotional part of the brain, not in the rational part of the brain. And so... the problem [of divorce] is often presented as a rational problem [when, in some sense,] it's more of an emotional problem with practical overlays.

Adam: Right. I imagine that part of what makes divorce so challenging is that you don't really know where the ground is. One week, you might feel okay, and then facts change, and the next week everything is totally different. That probably creates a kind of disequilibrium.

Katherine: Yes. You define yourself in some ways by your marriage…. [and then] you have to start to redefine yourself in the world… and that's very disorienting, right? It's like the loss of a loved one, like the loss of a parent. *Who am I in the world, if I am not the wife or the husband of this other person?* Especially for a person who did not choose the divorce, that redefinition can be very hard.

Adam: Speaking of redefinition, how does the process of reordering your life begin? Like, can you walk us through the process, from when someone comes into your office? Where are they at, and what happens going forward from there?

Katherine: That's a very big question! When people come in, they're getting divorced… they chose it, or they didn't choose it. Either way they're not really sure what it means. Think of when you got married. I'm guessing here, but you probably planned your wedding, you had a reception -- who's going to be on the guest list, who's not going to be on the guest list, what are your flowers going to be, what's the dress going to be, what are the colors of the napkins...

But do we ever think about the details of a divorce? The answer to this question for most people is a resounding, *no!*

We never think about that. How would our relationship…
be different? What decisions would need to be made about
our stuff, our healthcare, about the relationship between us
and our parents? The only time people ever really think
about those scenarios is when they do a pre-nuptial
agreement. So, in coming apart, you have to start thinking
about how you came together and what it means to have
come together… you need to understand that in order to
make decisions about coming apart.

There are generally three big areas that people need to
resolve…

Parenting. Parenting divides into two pieces. One is
decision making. How will people make parenting
decisions? Not, like, *what's for dinner?* but medical
decisions, education decisions, stuff like that… really big,
general parenting decisions… is one person is going to
make them? Will they make them together? Or will they
divide up into spheres of influence -- for example, one
person gets decision making on secular education, the other
person gets decision making religious education? Or one
person makes educational decisions and the other medical
decisions.

The other [parenting issue] is timesharing: *Where will the
kids be, when? What is that going to look like in regular
time? Will that be different for special time, like holidays
and vacations and weekends? What will that look like? And
how will that plan change as the children grow up?*

The second area is **assets and liabilities**. The couple needs
to figure out what they have, what [those assets] are worth,
what they owe, and how they are going to divide that up.

The third big area is **cash flow**. *What does it cost to live your life? What's it going to cost to live separately? What do you anticipate your income is going to be? Will there be cash flow between you, and [if so] how do we characterize that?* [The couple needs] to make a plan so that each of them will be okay and cover their bills. That's part of what we work towards in Collaborative and in mediation, too… creating a forward-looking cash flow plan that makes sense.

Those are the three big areas; the supporting areas could be life insurance and health insurance and estate planning and things like that.

So that's sort of like "The What" they need to decide, between the time that they *decide* to get divorced and the time that they *get* divorced. Those are the substantive conversations.

Before they engage in The What discussions, they need to decide "How" those decisions will be made. The first [element] is… how are they going to make those decisions? What process will they choose to identify the issues that they need to resolve?

In mediation, they sit together in a room with a mediator, who facilitates the conversation between the two of them. Typically, they will consult with attorneys outside their rooms, although sometimes [the attorneys] come in.

Or they can work Collaboratively, where they both have attorneys, and by agreement of all participants the attorneys are disqualified from litigating. So everybody has 100%

skin in the game to settle. In the Collaborative process we have the opportunity to work with an interdisciplinary team to support all the different aspects [at play when] families come apart and transition to becoming a binuclear family.

The way I think of divorce is really sort of the untangling of different colored yarns in a knitting basket that a kitten has gotten into and jumbled all together. We have to untangle the financial from the parenting, from the emotion, from the extended family, from the neighbors, from the religious community… you've got the yellow and green and the red and the purple. And we're trying to untangle those from each other.

The problem is that, as you pull on the financial (the "red" string), you're really tangled up with the emotional (the "blue" string). Right? It's a terrible knot. It's like, back and forth and back and forth and back and forth. So, the idea of the [Collaborative] team is to approach the yellow string with yellow expertise and the red string with red expertise and the blue string with blue expertise… to help people untangle in the least disruptive, most constructive way possible, so they have an opportunity to build a new relationship rather than just sort of tear apart the old one.

Adam: Right. To continue with your metaphor, it sounds like the more traditional approaches just take out the scissors.

Katherine: That's right. That's good. I'm going to use that.

Adam: Well, so, the people who've read your book are now somewhat familiar with now the concepts of Collaborative Divorce. But they might have hesitations...

what are the common fears people have regarding this kind of process, and what do you say in response?

Katherine: I think for most people, once they understand it, it makes sense to them.

Some people might think it's expensive – *we're going to have all of these professionals in the room?* But it's not more expensive compared to traditional litigation. In litigation, [you're likely to] settle before the judge hands down a decision. Often, people settle on the courthouse steps on the eve of trial or after a day of trial... after expensive appearances in court and extensive discovery. The fact that you're going to settle doesn't mean it's going to be just a couple of conversations between lawyers and *hey, we're done!*

Another concern that people sometimes have is [the fear that] the Collaborative process will be time consuming. People [worry] it's just going to take a long time. By that, I think they mean they fear it will be painful. And here's the thing. It IS going to be painful. It's going to be painful, no matter what. I mean, divorce is hard even for the person who wants to divorce.

When I walked down the aisle at my first marriage, did I think *well, this is going to go 10 years, then I am going to dump this guy and put my kids through a divorce, and it will be torture between us?* I was thinking *this is wonderful, this is just great. We are going to have a family together and love each other.* Making the decision to divorce was painful and going through it was hard. And I think that it makes sense to take the time to carefully transition your family.

Sometimes people think: *this sounds good, but I will never convince my spouse*. I don't really understand that, because if it sounds good to one person, it should sound good to both people. There's a theory called __reactive devaluation__, which says that, *if I'm in conflict with you, anything that I say as a suggestion, you're not going to like it, even if you said it five minutes ago*. If you say *let's order Chinese*, and I am in conflict with you, and I say, *you know, I don't really want that. How about we get Italian?* And then, finally, I say *all right, let's get Chinese*. Then you say, *no, I don't want Chinese* [just] because I said it!

Obviously, that's a very extreme example; it doesn't usually work like that. Sometimes, I think people think that if they suggest to their husband or wife that they do Collaborative, [the other person] is going to feel like there is a trick. *You're trying to trick me into this.* When clients come in -- and they either haven't told their spouse that they want a divorce, or they've talked about divorce, but they haven't picked lawyers. When they decide that [they want to do] Collaborative, we have a conversation. I ask: *Am I going to tell your spouse, or are you going to tell him or her?*

I think it's much better if the person who wants the Collaborative Divorce goes home and says to their spouse, *hey, I went to talk to this lawyer, and she told me about this process; it looks really interesting to me. Why don't you check it out?* as opposed to me writing a letter. A lawyer's letter lands heavily no matter how nicely it is written.

Adam: In terms of your emotional journey… you've helped people going through Collaborative Divorce as well as litigation… both kinds of cases. Can you tell a difference in terms of people's level of satisfaction or emotional equanimity?

Katherine: The Collaborative process, I think, [leads to] fewer post divorce problems. Does that mean that there are no problems? It does not mean that. It does not mean that people don't change their mind… or agree to things that they really don't want to agree to, just to get it over with, and then they regret and refuse to do what they agreed to do during the Collaborative sessions. I mean, we try not to have that happen. We have a place for them to discuss things. And in a kind of ironic way, we lawyers rarely hear from them, because the interdisciplinary process [helps them work things out]. They can go to the coach… or have a child specialist or financial person assist.

So they rarely, in my experience, really have post-divorce problems. Whereas in a litigation, people [often white knuckle it until] they agree on the courthouse steps. They are running out of money. They are absolutely terrified about what's going to happen. They agree because they just want to stop the pain of not agreeing. *Stop torturing me* is not a good reason to agree. And the divorce process can be a torturous one. In *Eat Pray Love*, Elizabeth Gilbert [the author] writes in the beginning of the book, *"I pity the poor readers who have had to go through a New York divorce."*

Now, having said that… sometimes difficult people have problems because they are difficult. And sometimes people still settle because they feel external pressure to do so and live to regret the terms.

Adam: Right. There is only so much the process itself can do.

Katherine: Yes.

Adam: It seems like the success of this process hinges on the interdisciplinary people you bring in, right? How do you find those people? I mean, do you have go-to people you use – people that you've vetted? How does it work with all these different cooks in the kitchen?

Katherine: They are Collaboratively trained professionals and they bring tremendous depth to the effectiveness of the Collaborative process. On the other hand, in some cases if you have sensitive, psychologically savvy and financially aware attorneys, it can work with just the attorneys.

Having said that, [it's quite useful] to be able to work with a trusted team of people who have been trained, who I can recommend, who I know will work well with me and my clients and who have been supportive before.

Adam: That's cool. That's excellent. It seems like, over time, you probably get better and better with the process. Like, the more divorces you do, the easier it is to anticipate potential problems and head them off and to find the right team. Is that right?

Katherine: The longer you work in this way, hopefully, the better you get at it. One thing that I have learned is: it never helps to argue with the other client. I mean, how is that ever going to work out well? [Let's say a couple] comes into a Collaborative meeting, and the wife says, *I really want to stay in the house, because I feel like it's* *really important for me and for the kids, and we should stay there indefinitely because that feels right to me.* So as the husband's attorney, you think to yourself: *well, that's really an unreasonable position.*

Am I going to try to convince her otherwise? What could I possibly say to convince her otherwise? Can you think of anything I could possibly say to the wife in that moment as her husband's lawyer that would have her stop and think she might be wrong? Nothing!

Sometimes, by not arguing, you can really gain a lot of trust just by trying instead to understand what she is saying. *I understand it's really important for you to stay in the house; it really feels really crucial.* If I say that, instead of trying to argue, [it often leads to a much better outcome]. It takes time and experience to realize that, if you don't argue, it doesn't mean you lose. Like: not arguing the point doesn't mean you lose it! It just means you don't dig yourself further into a hole in that particular moment. That particular kind of thing, it takes practice.

Adam: Yeah. It's almost like... I don't want to say "psychological ninjutsu," because you're not playing a trick... you're really just trying to empathize, to start with empathy and then reflect.

Katherine: Absolutely.

Adam: *Here's what you're feeling, and here's what you're saying.* And I feel like there's a real starvation -- a need to be "listened to" in the world, especially among people who are going through a divorce. They feel like *no one is* *listening to me, no one is hearing me.* So, having their emotions reflected back can be powerful?

Katherine: Right… People often think *if you just understood what I was saying, and how I am coming from such a good place, you would just agree with me, and we wouldn't be arguing, but you're not listening to me.* And the other person thinks, *no, you are not listening to me!* And the truth is that neither is listening.

Adam: Well, it seems like there's more and more research coming out to support that point. Have you heard of Nonviolent Communication?

Katherine: Yeah. Sure. That's Marshall Rosenberg, right?

Adam: Yeah.

Katherine: Right. There's another thing called Powerful Non-defensive Communication started by a woman named Sharon Strand Ellison, which is really good. She actually has a whole thing on non-defensive parenting… like how to talk to your kids in a way that doesn't dis-empower them, but also gets your point across. I would recommend that you buy the CD and listen to her read it rather than read the book, because a lot of it has to do with the intonation of your voice and, when she demonstrates it on the CD, you get it a lot more than if you read it.

Adam: That makes a lot of sense… [when you're trying to empathize] it's very difficult to come across like you're not playing a trick or something. You know what I mean?

Katherine: I think I do. This is what I do every day. I think that there are [key elements that are relevant]… one is the way you say [something], and the other is what I call the conflict dynamic.

Every couple develops a conflict dynamic. And it's not just couples. We have this with our parents, with our children, with our close friends or neighbors. It's a pattern. A client [looking at her conflict dynamic with her husband might reflect]: *He says something, I say something. He responds to what I said, and then if I say the thing that's in my head at that moment, I could literally write out for the next 20 or 30 minutes exactly what he would say and what I would say, and what he would say, and what I would say, and then we will both walk away frustrated, unhappy, and angry.*

And that conflict pattern… part of what we do in the Collaborative process and mediation is to interrupt the conflict pattern, so we end up in a more constructive place, where each person understands the other better, and we can walk away feeling like we've made progress.

You [also] really have to be coming from [a place of] genuine curiosity, and not like, *I can't imagine what you were thinking about the lunch when you packed it* but rather *I was really curious about what you packed in the lunch, because I wouldn't have done it that way and I'd really like to know what you were thinking about, because maybe I could do it that way, too.* You see how different that was in terms of the intonation?

Adam: Okay. I love that. That's really interesting. And you're right. Intonation matters a lot. Isn't it something like

80% of how you communicate with people has to do with body language -- the subtle inflections and tones of voice. The actual substance of what you say obviously matters, but these other things also matter and potentially more so.

Katherine: Yes, absolutely.

Adam: We shouldn't make this interview too long! But I was wondering... is there anything specific to New York or New York's version of Collaborative law that you wanted to talk about? And do you have any last words of wisdom for people, as they're thinking about getting divorce or doing Collaborative or working with you?

Katherine: About working with me?

Adam: Yeah.

Katherine: I don't want to make this too much of a hard sell. I mean, I really think that people should work with someone with whom they feel comfortable. If you want to go back to the beginning of this year, I wrote something called Gorillas Don't Make Good Lawyers. And the reason I did that is because, if you hire someone who you think is going to be "tough enough" to handle your ex, then that tough person is going to be handling you, too in that same tough way. You need to find someone with whom you feel comfortable... who really has your back and whose presence will help you speak in an authentic way in the meetings... I think it really pays to try to be your best self when you are getting divorced.

Go to the higher road rather than lower road. And sometimes people feel: *if I take the high road, then I am vulnerable*. Right? Because we have all kinds of expressions like *nice guys finish last* that indicate that doing the right thing is a weak thing. And I think that that's really, really false. It's especially false when you're in a conflict where relationships matter and divorce when you have children. If you think that your marriage was a mistake, then think about what that means about your life and about the time you spent with this person. Instead of thinking this was a mistake, try *this was a relationship that ran its course and ended, leaving us with these beautiful children, leaving us with these wonderful memories, leaving us with these adventures we had together, these things I learned from you...* as opposed to this being a mistake.

When you think back on the divorce process, if you were your worst self... if you just allowed yourself to give into your lowest, basest, most primitive instincts... You're going to hate yourself, not just him or her... and that just makes it so much worse. There's book called The Good Karma Divorce written by Michele Lowrance who was a family judge or former family judge and a child of divorce, and she'd been divorced three times herself. She's had a lot of experience.

In The Good Karma Divorce, she makes that point that you should write out who you want to be and what your core values are and be that person as much as you can. Write it down, like a mission statement for yourself. *This is who I want to be in this divorce.*

Sometimes we run into what I call the "chump factor." *I would do this, but it would mean I was giving into you. And even though I don't really mind doing this thing, I don't want to give into you, because that would make me a chump.* That's like the opposite of what I'm talking about -- get away from the chump factor. Be your better self. Even if you are the only one doing that, you are going to get a better result, and it doesn't make you vulnerable to be your better self.

Adam: That makes a lot of sense. It's almost like a philosophical point of view. We have one life to live, right? And we can't control the past, we can't control the future… but you *can* control how you are in the present. So, if you can always focus on your core values and what you would like to happen, ultimately, aggregately, it's going to work out well for you?

Katherine: Yes. That's right. Exactly. Like: what's really important… to you, your kids, your safety, and not the small stuff?

You know, I have a friend who has a friend getting divorced in another city. Our mutual friend asked if I would talk to her, and I agreed. We had this conversation, and she said, *so here we are here, we have divided everything up, and now we're just talking about the stuff in the house. What do you think I should do?* And I said, *I think you should just let him have it.* And she said *what?* I said, *it's stuff, right? It's towels. Buy more towels. Don't you win, in some ways, by letting him have the towels and by being generous? He'll feel better about it, and you can just buy more towels.* That led into a whole conversation about the conflict dynamic, about why he wanted these towels in the first place. Guess what? It turns out it is not the towels that are the problem. It is so easy to get drawn into the fight about the towels rather than look for what is really going on.

Adam: Yeah.

Katherine: Right. It's like, if you stay focused on what's really important, then you don't get into these dogfights over the towels. [She realized] *yeah, they are pink towels, what does he want them for...? You know what? You are totally right. It's not the towels.*

Adam: Not the towels. That's fantastic. That's great. I think it's a good moral to close this interview on. Focus on the big picture and on being a good person throughout this experience, which is unpleasant -- as you said, it sucks -- but you can make it suck less.

Katherine: If you like how you are in the process, it's going to suck less. And that's something that you have control over. You don't have control over the other person, you don't have control over so many things in life, but you do have control over yourself.

Adam: That's right. Well, Thank you, Katherine. This has been an awesome interview.

Katherine: Good. It's been fun.

Resources in New York for Information on <u>Collaborative Divorce</u>

- <u>New York Association of Collaborative Professionals</u> **(New York, United States)**

- <u>Adirondack Alternative Divorce Solutions, Inc. (AADS, Inc.)</u> **(New York, New York, United States)**

- <u>Association of Collaborative Lawyers of Rockland-Westchester</u> **(New York, United States)**

- <u>CNY Collaborative Family Law Professionals, Inc.</u> **(Syracuse Area, New York, United States)**

- <u>Collaborative Divorce Association of the Capital District</u> **(New York, United States)**

- <u>Collaborative Divorce Group of Westchester and Putnam</u> **(New York, United States)**

- <u>Collaborative Divorce Team of the Hudson Valley</u> **(New York, United States)**

- <u>Collaborative Law Association of the Rochester Area, Inc.</u> **(Rochester Area, New York, United States)**

- [Collaborative North](#) (**Northern Capital District of NY, New York, United States**)

- [Finger Lakes Collaborative Law Association](#) (**New York, United States**)

- [Hudson Valley Collaborative Divorce & Dispute Resolution Association](#) (**New York, United States**)

- [Ithaca Area Collaborative Law Professionals](#) (**New York, United States**)

- [LGBTQ Collaborative Professionals of NYC](#) (**The Five Boroughs of New York City, New York, United States**)

- [Mid-Hudson Valley Collaborative Divorce Professionals](#) (**New York, United States**)

- [Mohawk Valley Association of Collaborative Law Professionals, Inc.](#) (**New York, United States**)

- [New York Civil Collaborative Group](#) (**New York, United States**)

- [Rockland Collaborative Law Network](#) (**New York, United States**)

- [Staten Island Collaborative Law Group](#) (**Richmond County, Staten Island, New York, United States**)

- **Western New York Collaborative Law Professionals, Ltd.** (New York, United States)

Disclaimer for "The New Yorker's Guide to Collaborative Divorce"

You understand that this book is not intended as a substitution for a consultation with an attorney. Requesting this book or viewing the information in it does not create an attorney-client relationship with the Miller Law Group, Katherine Eisold Miller, PC, Katherine Miller or any of its attorneys. To obtain legal advice about your divorce matter, please engage the services of the Miller Law Group, Katherine Eisold Miller, PC or another law firm of your choice.

THE MILLER LAW GROUP AND KATHERINE EISOLD MILLER, PC, ARE PROVIDING "THE NEW YORKER'S GUIDE TO COLLABORATIVE DIVORCE" (HEREAFTER REFERRED TO AS "BOOK") AND ITS CONTENTS ON AN "AS IS" BASIS AND MAKES NO REPRESENTATIONS OR WARRANTIES OF ANY KIND WITH RESPECT TO THIS BOOK OR ITS CONTENTS. THE MILLER LAW GROUP AND KATHERINE EISOLD MILLER, PC DISCLAIMS ALL SUCH REPRESENTATIONS AND WARRANTIES, INCLUDING FOR EXAMPLE WARRANTIES OF MERCHANTABILITY AND FITNESS FOR A PARTICULAR PURPOSE. IN ADDITION, THE MILLER LAW GROUP AND KATHERINE EISOLD MILLER, PC DO NOT REPRESENT OR WARRANT THAT THE INFORMATION ACCESSIBLE VIA THIS BOOK IS ACCURATE, COMPLETE OR CURRENT.

Neither the Miller Law Group, Katherine Eisold Miller, PC nor any authors, contributors, or other representatives will be liable for damages arising out of or in connection with the use of this book. This is a comprehensive limitation of liability that applies to all damages of any kind, including (without limitation) compensatory; direct, indirect or consequential damages; loss of data, income or profit; loss of or damage to property, claims of third parties and punitive damages.

www.ingramcontent.com/pod-product-compliance
Lightning Source LLC
Chambersburg PA
CBHW070546030426
42337CB00016B/2375